A Circle in the Dark

A Circle in the Dark

Daily Meditations for Advent

RACHAEL A. KEEFE

WIPF *&* STOCK · Eugene, Oregon

Wipf & Stock
An Imprint of Wipf and Stock Publishers
199 W. 8th Ave., Suite 3
Eugene, OR 97401

www.wipfandstock.com

ISBN 13: 978-1-61097-339-7

Manufactured in the U.S.A.

For Erika
who reminds me that there is always light
no matter the depth of the darkness.

Contents

Acknowledgments ix
Introduction xi
Prologue xv

Week One   Hope 1
Week Two   Peace 23
Week Three   Joy 45
Week Four   Love 65
Christmas 86

Reader's Guide 91

Scripture Index 105

Acknowledgments

This book is the result of my Doctor of Ministry work at Andover Newton Theological School. Thank you Merle Jordan for strongly encouraging me to go back to school and for all your support through the writing process. This book might not have been written if Beth Nordbeck had not suggested it. Thank you. I also thank Beth for her patience and encouragement especially in my reluctance with the less poetic aspects of the work. I must also thank Mary Luti for her reminders to step beyond where I am most comfortable. I am also grateful to Jed Rardin for his unfailing collegial support and encouragement and willingness to use some of the poems in worship early on. Of course there are many others to whom I owe much gratitude—Sharon Thornton for her unbridled enthusiasm; Tim Thomas for his assurances that I have a gift worthy of sharing; for Erika Sanborne for her patience and company along the way; and for the numerous friends and colleagues who have offered encouragement, requests for more, and prayers throughout the writing process.

Introduction

We live in a world full of noise and busyness. It is easy to forget that the church has a different message to offer to the overburdened, overtired individual and to get lost in the chaos of secular living. This feeling of being overwhelmed can be magnified during Advent. The lights and sounds, memories and longings, traditions and ritual—all vying for our attention. As we begin the liturgical year, we may feel the effects of Advent's long history. It stretches back to its penitential roots and carries a somber weight while reaching toward joyous anticipation of Christmas. There are hints of darkness as we explore the areas of our personal lives or aspects of our faith communities that are not quite ready for Christ to come again. On the other hand, the Light of Christ shines, invitingly, a beacon for all who seek it.

From my early days in ministry, through community, parish, and healthcare settings, one question has been repeatedly asked of me: "I have everything I thought I would ever want—good job, great spouse, healthy kids, nice house, etc.—why do I feel so empty?" The people who have uttered these words in the privacy of my office, have almost always been the leaders of the church, the women and men who make things happen in the church and in the wider community. They have come with such a deep longing for meaning and purpose in their lives. It is for them as much as for those whose needs seem closer to the surface, that I offer a way of carrying an intentional Advent practice out of the worship service into everyday living.

The following pages may seem different from some more familiar Advent devotional material. It is divided into four weeks, each with one of the traditional themes for Advent—Hope, Peace, Joy, and Love—with the addition of Christmas Eve and Christmas Day. Each day has a scripture reading or two which is found somewhere within the Daily Lectionary Readings for Advent. Since the Daily Lectionary has a two-year cycle and I have written for one Advent season, I chose the readings that spoke to me. Sometimes the link between the scripture and the poem is clear and other times there is only a common theme, or maybe both the scripture verses and the poem point the reader toward the same truth. But I encourage you to attend to the scriptures; it is through them that we are tied to the community of faith with its long history of loving and yearning for God and being loved, forgiven, and shaped by God. So read them as closely as you read the poems.

You might also notice that a closing or summarizing prayer (often a predictable part of a daily devotional) is absent. This was an intentional choice. Sometimes, the poems themselves are prayers, deeply personal desires to communicate and connect with God, and adding an additional concluding prayer would be redundant. Other times, the voice of the poem is less prayerful but may evoke prayers from the reader. I did not want to prescribe the content of a prayer for you, the reader, but to allow further prayer or deeper reflection as you choose or are so moved.

I hope that as you read these poems, you will encounter Christ in a new way. I titled this book *A Circle in the Dark* because I think it is easy for all of us to get lost along the way. Advent can be a troubling time of year with all the pressures of a consumerist society in hard economic times, the strains of family obligations, and the pervasive pursuit of the mythic Rockwellian Christmas. The lighted Advent Candles create a small circle of Hope, Peace, Joy and Love that symbolize all that we yearn for (and all that is yearning for us) in the season. It is a simple circle of light in the potentially dark chaos of the world that invites us into another way of being.

These poems name the darkness and light of my own experiences as one who seeks an intentional relationship with God and to make meaning in the face of suffering. Sometimes I raise the questions of my heart or share the echoes of another person's pain. At other times I point in the direction of mystery or wonder or awe in the nature of God and the amazing resiliency of the human spirit. You may also hear words of deep lament as I am struck by our capacity to do harm to ourselves, one another, and our world. My hope is that as you read, you will feel a resonance in your own spirit that will provoke you to claim more fully your rightful place in the Light.

For those who would like some guidance in this regard, there is a Reader's Guide at the end of the book. It offers questions for each poem that may lead you to further reflection on your own or with others. I do not wish to limit the use of these poems. They can be used for personal, daily devotional reading to provide a depth of meaning to your experience of Advent. They can be used in worship services and Advent study groups. Be creative. But do not be intimidated by poetry. There is no right or wrong meaning for any poem. And what I thought, as the writer, is far less important that what you feel, think, and experience as you read.

In the pages that follow, I have pointed toward breathing new life into old rituals and uncovering meaning and embracing mystery. May your Advent season be filled with wonder and awe as you step into the Light of Hope, Peace, Joy, and Love.

Prologue

Arise, shine; for your light has come, and the glory of the Lord has risen upon you. For darkness shall cover the earth, and thick darkness the peoples; but the Lord will arise upon you, and his glory will appear over you. Nations shall come to your light, and kings to the brightness of your dawn. Lift up your eyes and look around; they all gather together, they come to you; your sons shall come from far away, and your daughters shall be carried on their nurses' arms.

—Isaiah 60:1–4

A CIRCLE IN THE DARK

Four candles create a circle of light
    Advent—the season of promise.

        The promise of hope . . .
            How?
                When a girl swallows lethal pills
                or another shoots heroine into her arm
                or another lives on the streets?
            I light the first candle and wonder where I am.

        The promise of peace . . .
            For whom?
                The rape victim
                or the runaway
                or the juvenile thief?
            I light the second candle and wonder where God is.

        The promise of joy . . .
            Where?
                In the family filled with grief
                or the one burdened by hunger
                or the one huddled in the shelter?
            I light the third candle and wonder where the light is.

        The promise of love . . .
            When?
                In the dark of loneliness
                or the cold of fear
                or the fire of hate?
            I light the fourth candle and wonder why.

The promise of Emanuel . . .
God with us
even now
in the darkness
and the chaos
and the noise.
I will light the Christ candle and wonder . . .

Hope

Let your steadfast love, O Lord, be upon us, even as we
hope in you.

—Psalm 33:22

SUNDAY

In the days of King Herod of Judea, there was a priest named Zechariah, who belonged to the priestly order of Abijah. His wife was a descendant of Aaron, and her name was Elizabeth. Both of them were righteous before God, living blamelessly according to all the commandments and regulations of the Lord. But they had no children, because Elizabeth was barren, and both were getting on in years. Once when he was serving as priest before God and his section was on duty, he was chosen by lot, according to the custom of the priesthood, to enter the sanctuary of the Lord and offer incense. Now at the time of the incense offering, the whole assembly of the people was praying outside. Then there appeared to him an angel of the Lord, standing at the right side of the altar of incense. When Zechariah saw him, he was terrified; and fear overwhelmed him. But the angel said to him, "Do not be afraid, Zechariah, for your prayer has been heard. Your wife Elizabeth will bear you a son, and you will name him John. You will have joy and gladness, and many will rejoice at his birth, for he will be great in the sight of the Lord. He must never drink wine or strong drink; even before his birth he will be filled with the Holy Spirit. He will turn many of the people of Israel to the Lord their God. With the spirit and power of Elijah he will go before him, to turn the hearts of parents to their children, and the disobedient to the wisdom of the righteous, to make ready a people prepared for the Lord." Zechariah said to the angel, "How will I know that this is so? For I am an old man, and my wife is getting on in years." The angel replied, "I am Gabriel. I stand in the presence of God, and I have been sent to speak to you and to bring you this good news. But now, because you did not believe my words, which will be fulfilled in their time, you will become mute, unable to speak, until the day these things occur." Meanwhile the people were waiting for Zechariah, and wondered at his delay in the sanctuary. When he did come out, he could not speak to them, and they realized that he had seen a vision in the sanctuary. He kept motioning to them and remained unable to speak. When his time of service was ended, he went to his home. After those days his wife Elizabeth conceived, and for five months she remained in seclusion. She said, "This is what the Lord has done for me when he looked favorably on me and took away the disgrace I have endured among my people."

—Luke 1:5–25

RE-VISION

A simple man in service to You
had all but given up his hope for more
until You startled him into silence,
filling his doubt with promise.

Did You blame him for his fear?
No priest expects routine to be visionary.
A simple offering seldom brings angels
while angels always bring "fear not"
a little too late.

When Zechariah lost his words
did he hear Yours more clearly?
How long did he cling to doubt
before he saw the light?

Today, Your people are lost in tradition
rarely expecting more than routine
while hope slips into darkness.

Silence our distracting disbelief.
Disrupt our routine with startling visions
allowing us to re-vision You.

We wait with Zechariah.

MONDAY

Alas for you who desire the day of the Lord! Why do you want the day of the Lord? It is darkness, not light; as if someone fled from a lion, and was met by a bear; or went into the house and rested a hand against the wall, and was bitten by a snake. Is not the day of the Lord darkness, not light, and gloom with no brightness in it? I hate, I despise your festivals, and I take no delight in your solemn assemblies. Even though you offer me your burnt offerings and grain offerings, I will not accept them; and the offerings of well-being of your fatted animals I will not look upon. Take away from me the noise of your songs; I will not listen to the melody of your harps. But let justice roll down like waters, and righteousness like an ever-flowing stream. Did you bring to me sacrifices and offerings the forty years in the wilderness, O house of Israel? You shall take up Sakkuth your king, and Kaiwan your star-god, your images, which you made for yourselves; therefore I will take you into exile beyond Damascus, says the Lord, whose name is the God of hosts.

—Amos 5:18–27

In the sixth month the angel Gabriel was sent by God to a town in Galilee called Nazareth, to a virgin engaged to a man whose name was Joseph, of the house of David. The virgin's name was Mary. And he came to her and said, "Greetings, favored one! The Lord is with you." But she was much perplexed by his words and pondered what sort of greeting this might be. The angel said to her, "Do not be afraid, Mary, for you have found favor with God. And now, you will conceive in your womb and bear a son, and you will name him Jesus. He will be great, and will be called the Son of the Most High, and the Lord God will give to him the throne of his ancestor David. He will reign over the house of Jacob forever, and of his kingdom there will be no end." Mary said to the angel,

"How can this be, since I am a virgin?" The angel said to her, "The Holy Spirit will come upon you, and the power of the Most High will overshadow you; therefore the child to be born will be holy; he will be called Son of God. And now, your relative Elizabeth in her old age has also conceived a son; and this is the sixth month for her who was said to be barren. For nothing will be impossible with God." Then Mary said, "Here am I, the servant of the Lord; let it be with me according to your word." Then the angel departed from her.

—Luke 1:26–38

THEN AND NOW

empty praises
noisy songs
meaningless sacrifices
pointless offerings
false gods
forgotten justice
abandoned righteousness
      a people in exile

        half-hearted prayers
        whispered songs
        infrequent sacrifices
        insufficient offerings
        inadequate gods
        deficient justice
        superficial righteousness
a people lost

an angel visit
a young woman afraid
a life-changing offer
doubtful hesitation
affirming explanation
thoughtful silence
active acceptance
      prophecy fulfilled

        hidden despair
        glittering images
        untold longing
        frenetic activity

unheard stories
unknown stillness
echoing doubts
elapsed promise

a courageous girl
accepts responsibility
changes everything
inviting exiles
rescuing the lost
replacing doubt
invoking possibility
Emanuel then

and now
sing out loud
remember God-with-us
offering life
instilling meaning
embodying justice
living righteousness
a people reclaimed

TUESDAY

See, the day is coming, burning like an oven, when all the arrogant and all evildoers will be stubble; the day that comes shall burn them up, says the Lord of hosts, so that it will leave them neither root nor branch. But for you who revere my name the sun of righteousness shall rise, with healing in its wings. You shall go out leaping like calves from the stall. And you shall tread down the wicked, for they will be ashes under the soles of your feet, on the day when I act, says the Lord of hosts. Remember the teaching of my servant Moses, the statutes and ordinances that I commanded him at Horeb for all Israel. Lo, I will send you the prophet Elijah before the great and terrible day of the Lord comes. He will turn the hearts of parents to their children and the hearts of children to their parents, so that I will not come and strike the land with a curse.

—Malachi 4:1–6

In the fifteenth year of the reign of Emperor Tiberius, when Pontius Pilate was governor of Judea, and Herod was ruler of Galilee, and his brother Philip ruler of the region of Ituraea and Trachonitis, and Lysanias ruler of Abilene, during the high priesthood of Annas and Caiaphas, the word of God came to John son of Zechariah in the wilderness. He went into all the region around the Jordan, proclaiming a baptism of repentance for the forgiveness of sins, as it is written in the book of the words of the prophet Isaiah, "The voice of one crying out in the wilderness: 'Prepare the way of the Lord, make his paths straight. Every valley shall be filled, and every mountain and hill shall be made low, and the crooked shall be made straight, and the rough ways made smooth; and all flesh shall see the salvation of God.'"

—Luke 3:1–6

PREPARE YE THE WAY

In answer to prayer
I've traded ocean for mountains
        constant motion for deep stillness
        familiar rhythm for barely audible sound

Unlike the dark nights I've left behind
this night sings of light
thousands of stars testify to their Creator
        begging any attempt at denial
        pointing toward ancient promise and possibility

Amidst the boxes and books
a small wreath and five candles
bear the only witness to the season
in the remnants of my chaotic journey
yet to be unpacked

One purple candle burns on my table
recalling the hundreds of Advents past
How many hopes burned brightly
        in the wilderness
        desert
        high places
        low places
        oceans
        mountains
                from every corner of the earth
                a need for light

In this new place
my small candle burns in gratitude

and in prayer
for God-with-us
    to shine in the dark
        of war
        hunger
        sickness
        despair
        brokenness

Open the ears of all to the ocean's rhythm
    the mountain's stillness
        the song of the stars
the unending call to prepare the way

Emanuel shall come to us
    and fulfill the ancient promise and possibility
        that burst into the world
            one ordinary night
            and shines on

in a fragile flame
against the deep darkness of our world

Chaos gives way to stillness
and the path is made straight

WEDNESDAY

The days are surely coming, says the Lord, when I will fulfill the promise I made to the house of Israel and the house of Judah. In those days and at that time I will cause a righteous Branch to spring up for David; and he shall execute justice and righteousness in the land. In those days Judah will be saved and Jerusalem will live in safety. And this is the name by which it will be called: "The Lord is our righteousness."

—Jeremiah 33:14–16

BROKEN HOPE

Alone

darkness creeps closer than expected
pressing cold fingers on window panes
slipping through glass
touching restless dreams

disquiet in the night

    Unseen

       warring images deter sleep
       violence witnessed in battles
       familiar and foreign
       wound long after a body heals

       unrest wakens in the dark

         Isolated

           tears of grief flow unheard
           for the child lost
           despair grips harder
           in the absence of light

           hope breaks in silence

              Unknown

              days are surely coming

when light will burst through
with justice in hand
to fulfill a promise

Let us not walk in darkness too long

THURSDAY

The word of the Lord came to Jeremiah: Thus says the Lord: If any of you could break my covenant with the day and my covenant with the night, so that day and night would not come at their appointed time, only then could my covenant with my servant David be broken, so that he would not have a son to reign on his throne, and my covenant with my ministers the Levites. Just as the host of heaven cannot be numbered and the sands of the sea cannot be measured, so I will increase the offspring of my servant David, and the Levites who minister to me. The word of the Lord came to Jeremiah: Have you not observed how these people say, "The two families that the Lord chose have been rejected by him," and how they hold my people in such contempt that they no longer regard them as a nation? Thus says the Lord: Only if I had not established my covenant with day and night and the ordinances of heaven and earth, would I reject the offspring of Jacob and of my servant David and not choose any of his descendants as rulers over the offspring of Abraham, Isaac, and Jacob. For I will restore their fortunes, and will have mercy upon them.

—Jeremiah 33:19–26

HUMAN WAYS

You keep your covenant with day and night
and populate the earth with Your people.
The sands of the sea remain as immeasurable
as our capacity to turn from You.

Never has the world known peace
        which we seem to pursue with violence
        again and again
rejecting Your ways.

We blame You for destruction—
earthquake, fire, disease, tidal waves—
while we spill oil into the oceans,
strip forests of life,
poison the very air we breathe,
        not to mention valuing one life over another . . .

Yet, You remain steadfast in Your love for us.
Perhaps it is You who is waiting
with quiet anticipation
of something new.

Have mercy on us for our human ways.
Forgive our resistance to responsibility
and tendency to blame.

May Your waiting not be in vain.

FRIDAY

Thus says God, the Lord, who created the heavens and stretched them out, who spread out the earth and what comes from it, who gives breath to the people upon it and spirit to those who walk in it: I am the Lord, I have called you in righteousness, I have taken you by the hand and kept you; I have given you as a covenant to the people, a light to the nations, to open the eyes that are blind, to bring out the prisoners from the dungeon, from the prison those who sit in darkness. I am the Lord, that is my name; my glory I give to no other, nor my praise to idols. See, the former things have come to pass, and new things I now declare; before they spring forth, I tell you of them.

—Isaiah 42:5–9

A SONNET FOR HOPE

So complicated this journey of ours—
we stumble and fall, misread direction.
Seldom pausing to see purple flowers,
forgetting to seek beyond commotion.
When pain and suffering overwhelm us,
darkness descends and hope runs fast away.
Thinking ourselves alone with no one to trust
and no one to care, wisdom has no say—
until someone brings light, friend or stranger,
does not matter. A kind word, gentle touch
to remind us—One born in a manger
calls us by name. God gave the world so much—
we suffer, but we are cradled in love,
night broken open with light from above.

SATURDAY

Now the time came for Elizabeth to give birth, and she bore a son. Her neighbors and relatives heard that the Lord had shown his great mercy to her, and they rejoiced with her. On the eighth day they came to circumcise the child, and they were going to name him Zechariah after his father. But his mother said, "No; he is to be called John." They said to her, "None of your relatives has this name." Then they began motioning to his father to find out what name he wanted to give him. He asked for a writing tablet and wrote, "His name is John." And all of them were amazed. Immediately his mouth was opened and his tongue freed, and he began to speak, praising God. Fear came over all their neighbors, and all these things were talked about throughout the entire hill country of Judea.

—Luke 1:57–66

OF PROMISE AND GRACE

A barren life came to an end
with prophecy fulfilled.
Months of silence culminated in proclamation
echoing through the countryside.
Hope for Your people
took unexpected shape
in one who would clear the way for You.

Did Elizabeth wait patiently
or did she plead with You as
the years passed her by?

In the barren years, I let hope slide away
and allowed doubt to fill the silence.
Even in my longing for a word from You,
I would not have heard the ancient promise
nor the echoes of praise circling through the hills.
I stood on the cold, empty shore, encased in fog
trying to remember the glories of the sun,
believing I'd never see it again.

Elizabeth must have walked through
the depths of darkness
and carried the weight of despairing doubt
before You filled her with new life.
Perhaps she had lost her way before
You changed her direction.
What did she know in that moment?
Was it pure joy untainted by fear?
Or was it tempered with a hint
of the pain held off in days yet to come?

In this season of promise
let me stand in the light of Hope
undiminished by fear or pain
more rightly suited to other days.
As new life fills me,
teach me to sing its name
to fill the countryside
with echoes of praise
to ring through the hills.

Elizabeth, promise of God,
who watched and waited
through a lifetime of hope's ebb and flow
to give impossible birth to grace unforeseen
in a world with more than a little need.

The emptiness of many lives should come to an end
with prophecy being fulfilled once again.
Silence, doubt and fear ought to fade as praises rise
out of untold waiting.
Hope for Your people
takes unexpected shape, even now,
in all who would clear the way for You.

WEEK TWO

Peace

"Steadfast love and faithfulness will meet;
righteousness and peace will kiss each other."

—Psalm 85:10

SUNDAY

In days to come the mountain of the Lord's house shall be established as the highest of the mountains, and shall be raised above the hills; all the nations shall stream to it. Many peoples shall come and say, "Come, let us go up to the mountain of the Lord, to the house of the God of Jacob; that he may teach us his ways and that we may walk in his paths." For out of Zion shall go forth instruction, and the word of the Lord from Jerusalem. He shall judge between the nations, and shall arbitrate for many peoples; they shall beat their swords into plowshares, and their spears into pruning hooks; nation shall not lift up sword against nation, neither shall they learn war any more.

—Isaiah 2:2–4

ADVENT AGAIN

Christ is coming into the world
                              again.
                    Surely not here,
                         not now,
                              not again.

          The beaches are washed in grey
                    abandoned for the season
                              again.

          Children are bruised, beaten, broken
                         again and again.
                    And me along with them
                    as my demons rise to
                         Pull me under
                              again.

          My prayers are laments
                    as I try to believe that God
                         will come again.

          Carols burst from radio speakers
                    and trees light up again.

There was nothing extraordinary about that stable birth
               except that people noticed
                              again and
                              again and
                              again . . .

          God came into the world

to make life sacred once again.

I search the dark shore to find what I had lost again.
Through the night I walk
until the stars shine again.
The moon casts purple shadows
and there is light again.
I notice.
God will come again.
Here.
Now.
Emanuel.
Again.

MONDAY

Thus says the Lord: For three transgressions of Moab, and for four, I will not revoke the punishment; because he burned to lime the bones of the king of Edom. So I will send a fire on Moab, and it shall devour the strongholds of Kerioth, and Moab shall die amid uproar, amid shouting and the sound of the trumpet; I will cut off the ruler from its midst, and will kill all its officials with him, says the Lord. Thus says the Lord: For three transgressions of Judah, and for four, I will not revoke the punishment; because they have rejected the law of the Lord, and have not kept his statutes, but they have been led astray by the same lies after which their ancestors walked. So I will send a fire on Judah, and it shall devour the strongholds of Jerusalem. Thus says the Lord: For three transgressions of Israel, and for four, I will not revoke the punishment; because they sell the righteous for silver, and the needy for a pair of sandals—they who trample the head of the poor into the dust of the earth, and push the afflicted out of the way; father and son go in to the same girl, so that my holy name is profaned; they lay themselves down beside every altar on garments taken in pledge; and in the house of their God they drink wine bought with fines they imposed.

—Amos 2:1–8

There was a man sent from God, whose name was John. He came as a witness to testify to the light, so that all might believe through him. He himself was not the light, but he came to testify to the light. The true light, which enlightens everyone, was coming into the world. He was in the world, and the world came into being through him; yet the world did not know him. He came to what was his own, and his own people did not accept him. But to all who received him, who believed in his name, he gave power to become children of God, who were born, not of blood or of the will of the flesh or of the will of man, but of God.

—John 1:6–13

WORDS OF THE PROPHETS

chasing elusive dreams of wealth and glory
we worship silver and status
indulge in pleasure and foolish ways
all the while turning from You

while the words of the prophets
echo and fade into distant memory
as we reach for the glittery and glamorous
trinkets that shine briefly in our dark days

      yet You wait as consequences of our actions
      set destroying fires and deep hunger
      trails in their wake
      even as our own lies lead us further astray

      You wait—afire
      with proclamations of true light
      shining with promises of life
      for all who would believe in You

if we would but turn to You
all greedy illusions of power and wealth
would shatter at Your feet
and the words of the prophets

would call us back to Your way
we would set down our weapons
welcome our enemies
embrace Your sons and daughters

      wait patiently for us

who so need Your light
let us not be fooled any longer
fill us with peace

TUESDAY

The Lord said: Because these people draw near with their mouths and honor me with their lips, while their hearts are far from me, and their worship of me is a human commandment learned by rote; so I will again do amazing things with this people, shocking and amazing. The wisdom of their wise shall perish, and the discernment of the discerning shall be hidden. Ha! You who hide a plan too deep for the Lord, whose deeds are in the dark, and who say, "Who sees us? Who knows us?" You turn things upside down! Shall the potter be regarded as the clay? Shall the thing made say of its maker, "He did not make me"; or the thing formed say of the one who formed it, "He has no understanding"? Shall not Lebanon in a very little while become a fruitful field, and the fruitful field be regarded as a forest? On that day the deaf shall hear the words of a scroll, and out of their gloom and darkness the eyes of the blind shall see. The meek shall obtain fresh joy in the Lord, and the neediest people shall exult in the Holy One of Israel. For the tyrant shall be no more, and the scoffer shall cease to be; all those alert to do evil shall be cut off—those who cause a person to lose a lawsuit, who set a trap for the arbiter in the gate, and without grounds deny justice to the one in the right. Therefore thus says the Lord, who redeemed Abraham, concerning the house of Jacob: No longer shall Jacob be ashamed, no longer shall his face grow pale. For when he sees his children, the work of my hands, in his midst, they will sanctify my name; they will sanctify the Holy One of Jacob, and will stand in awe of the God of Israel. And those who err in spirit will come to understanding, and those who grumble will accept instruction.

—Isaiah 29:13–24

A QUIET LAMENT

Where is the understanding for those erring spirits?
When will Your name be sanctified?
Awe of You is surely absent in most places . . .

Day after day I look into their eyes
and see the hollow empty, places
left by the hands of others.
Who does this to our children?

Jacob grows more pale day by day
as little ones go hungry
or forgotten
or abused and misused.

Where is the joy and exultation
these meek and needy so desper-
ately call for?
There is no justice in their bruises
and no hope in their tears . . .

Where are the amazing things?
When will the blind see and the deaf hear?
Many hearts are surely far from You . . .
Some turn to me for wisdom
or justice or hope –
a flickering of light in blinding gloom.
I am but one . . .

Will You not put an end to ignorance
and madness?
Can you not shield the innocent,

protect the fragile ones before they break?

As You came to Jacob's aid,
come now.
Shock and amaze us all once again
lest we all fall into darkness.

Where is the understanding for our erring spirits?
When will we sanctify Your name?
Summon our hearts from far away . . .

WEDNESDAY

Your eyes will see the king in his beauty; they will behold a land that stretches far away. Your mind will muse on the terror: "Where is the one who counted? Where is the one who weighed the tribute? Where is the one who counted the towers?" No longer will you see the insolent people, the people of an obscure speech that you cannot comprehend, stammering in a language that you cannot understand. Look on Zion, the city of our appointed festivals! Your eyes will see Jerusalem, a quiet habitation, an immovable tent, whose stakes will never be pulled up, and none of whose ropes will be broken. But there the Lord in majesty will be for us a place of broad rivers and streams, where no galley with oars can go, nor stately ship can pass. For the Lord is our judge, the Lord is our ruler, the Lord is our king; he will save us.

—Isaiah 33:17–22

A PROMISE REMEMBERED

Long ago You promised a place of safety
solidly built for all Your children.
You would rule in beauty, security, and justice
with strength and understanding
for all who chose to live in You.

Yet, we are still searching for
the perfect city of power
and might. Indestructible.
Easily defended against
strangers and enemies—
a mighty fortress
to keep chosen ones safe.

But earthquakes, floods, fires and disease
dismantle structures put up with human hands
and storms wash away everything built on sand.
No thing lasts forever.
Strangers, enemies, and friends
appear the same if the distance is great enough.
No weapon ever leads to peace
just as no wall brings justice
or lasting security.

How is it that we have misunderstood for so long?
Or do we repeatedly forget—easily distracted by
our wants and desires,
impressed with our own power,
seeking to be greater than You,
thinking we are the potters and all is clay?
Yet, we remain so fragile—

so easily bent, bruised, and broken
at the whim of those who take power.

In this season of waiting, seeking, searching
reveal Yourself in us that we might
take up residence in Your city
of beauty, security, and justice
where strength and understanding
bring peace to all.

THURSDAY

Then the eyes of the blind shall be opened, and the ears of the deaf unstopped; then the lame shall leap like a deer, and the tongue of the speechless sing for joy. For waters shall break forth in the wilderness, and streams in the desert; the burning sand shall become a pool, and the thirsty ground springs of water; the haunt of jackals shall become a swamp, the grass shall become reeds and rushes.

—Isaiah 35:5-7

A VILLANELLE FOR ADVENT

I wait in darkness, longing for Your light.
Despair lingers, like jackals haunting me.
Come to me now; unleash Your peace tonight.

How soon will deserts bloom with Your delight
washing all fear in waters flowing free?
I wait in darkness, longing for Your light.

Wilderness and desert have filled my sight
long enough. I am hungry and thirsty—
Come to me now; unleash Your peace tonight.

Candles of hope and peace hold off the night
and herald the end of despondency.
I wait in darkness, longing for Your light.

When reeds and rushes grow, all will be right—
the lame will dance and all jackals will flee.
Come to me now; unleash Your peace tonight.

Keeping watch for You, I let go of fright
and anguish. Eagerly and prayerfully
I wait in darkness, longing for Your light;
Come to me now; unleash Your peace tonight.

FRIDAY

I can do nothing on my own. As I hear, I judge; and my judgment is just, because I seek to do not my own will but the will of him who sent me. If I testify about myself, my testimony is not true. There is another who testifies on my behalf, and I know that his testimony to me is true. You sent messengers to John, and he testified to the truth. Not that I accept such human testimony, but I say these things so that you may be saved. He was a burning and shining lamp, and you were willing to rejoice for a while in his light. But I have a testimony greater than John's. The works that the Father has given me to complete, the very works that I am doing, testify on my behalf that the Father has sent me. And the Father who sent me has himself testified on my behalf. You have never heard his voice or seen his form, and you do not have his word abiding in you, because you do not believe him whom he has sent.

—John 5:30–38

STORM WATCH

Outside
winds promise
early winter storms.
Clouds obscure
stars and moon,
casting no shadows,
creating yawning gloom.

Inside
candles cast
spectral light.
Memories draw near,
old pain and grief
awaken within,
obscuring today's hope.

The night
draws closer
touching me
with December's cold,
dark fingers
pushing away
tomorrow's promises.

I am haunted
by the emptiness
in an old friend's eyes.
He has lost his way,
fallen for illusions
and glittering idols—
unaware of deceit.

In the past
he held hope
when I could not.
He pointed to You
when I was adrift.
How far will he fall
before stumbling into You?

Cast Your light of peace
in this unsettling night.
Let the Truth shine
bright and warm,
chasing out all ghostly
despair and longing.
May no deceit linger here.

SATURDAY

On that day the branch of the Lord shall be beautiful and glorious, and the fruit of the land shall be the pride and glory of the survivors of Israel. Whoever is left in Zion and remains in Jerusalem will be called holy, everyone who has been recorded for life in Jerusalem, once the Lord has washed away the filth of the daughters of Zion and cleansed the bloodstains of Jerusalem from its midst by a spirit of judgment and by a spirit of burning. Then the Lord will create over the whole site of Mount Zion and over its places of assembly a cloud by day and smoke and the shining of a flaming fire by night. Indeed over all the glory there will be a canopy. It will serve as a pavilion, a shade by day from the heat, and a refuge and a shelter from the storm and rain.

—Isaiah 4:2–6

"Blessed be the Lord God of Israel, for he has looked favorably on his people and redeemed them. He has raised up a mighty savior for us in the house of his servant David, as he spoke through the mouth of his holy prophets from of old, that we would be saved from our enemies and from the hand of all who hate us. Thus he has shown the mercy promised to our ancestors, and has remembered his holy covenant, the oath that he swore to our ancestor Abraham, to grant us that we, being rescued from the hands of our enemies, might serve him without fear, in holiness and righteousness before him all our days. And you, child, will be called the prophet of the Most High; for you will go before the Lord to prepare his ways, to give knowledge of salvation to his people by the forgiveness of their sins. By the tender mercy of our God, the dawn from on high will break upon us, to give light to those who sit in darkness and in the shadow of death, to guide our feet into the way of peace." The child grew and became strong in spirit, and he was in the wilderness until the day he appeared publicly to Israel.

—Luke 1:68–80

A PRAYER FOR PEACE

Where is our refuge and our shelter?
We sit in darkness and the shadow of death.
War and violence fill our lives
     year after year.

     Is there no better way?

     Lord, in Your mercy,
     guide our feet in the way of peace.

We are awash in the bloodstains of judgment
and caught in the storms of hatred.
Ignorance and isolation separate us
     day after day.

     Is there no better way?

     Lord, in Your mercy,
     guide our feet in the way of peace.

We burn with shame and guilt
pleading with gods of our making
to offer us forgiveness and life
     hour by hour.

     Is there no better way?

     Lord, in Your mercy,
     guide our feet in the way of peace.

We are lost in the wilderness of fear

unable to recall the prophets of old.
We deceive ourselves
moment by moment.

Is there no better way?

Lord, in Your mercy,
guide our feet in the way of peace.

Let us sit in darkness no more!
Let us not cling to the shadows of death
or destruction or despair
for another minute!

There is a better way!

Lord, in Your mercy,
guide our feet in the way of peace.

Joy

"But let all who take refuge in you rejoice; let them ever sing for joy. Spread your protection over them, so that those who love your name may exult in you."

—Psalm 5:11

SUNDAY

Surely God is my salvation; I will trust, and will not be afraid, for the Lord God is my strength and my might; he has become my salvation. With joy you will draw water from the wells of salvation. And you will say in that day: Give thanks to the Lord, call on his name; make known his deeds among the nations; proclaim that his name is exalted. Sing praises to the Lord, for he has done gloriously; let this be known in all the earth. Shout aloud and sing for joy, O royal Zion, for great in your midst is the Holy One of Israel.

—Isaiah 12:2–6

THE THIRD CANDLE

A flickering fragile flame of joy
added to hope and peace
reminds me that this season of waiting
has purpose and direction
even as betrayal breaks into
my life yet
again.

The cold, leaden fog that deadens
sound and blurs edges
proves to be a product of weather
patterns
not a comment on my
emotional being
upset—yes,
again.

Trust shattered
doesn't have to splinter me.
There is more to this season
than cold and fog, chill and deception.
I can draw from a deeper well
that will dispel the dark
and heal the heartbreak
once again.

Soon, this circle will be complete.
Light will shine through
the broken places
bringing strength
and joy as praises rise through
lingering pain
to begin with You
again.

MONDAY

Sing aloud, O daughter Zion; shout, O Israel! Rejoice and exult with all your heart, O daughter Jerusalem! The Lord has taken away the judgments against you, he has turned away your enemies. The king of Israel, the Lord, is in your midst; you shall fear disaster no more. On that day it shall be said to Jerusalem: Do not fear, O Zion; do not let your hands grow weak. The Lord, your God, is in your midst, a warrior who gives victory; he will rejoice over you with gladness, he will renew you in his love; he will exult over you with loud singing as on a day of festival. I will remove disaster from you, so that you will not bear reproach for it. I will deal with all your oppressors at that time. And I will save the lame and gather the outcast, and I will change their shame into praise and renown in all the earth. At that time I will bring you home, at the time when I gather you; for I will make you renowned and praised among all the peoples of the earth, when I restore your fortunes before your eyes, says the Lord.

—Zephaniah 3:14–20

REGATHERING

Our hands have grown weak
and we are cloaked with shame.
We cast out more than we take in
and lock our doors in fear.
Disaster lurks in our belfries and vestries.
We claim victory and righteousness
as we sing praises familiar enough
to go unheard by our own ears.
If the Lord is in our midst,
why are we so fearful
of those who differ
    in belief
        in race
            in love
                in status
                    in health?
                        Surely we have lost our way . . .

The hour grows late and we are weary,
carrying burdens best left in stronger hands.
Can we not unlock our doors
and welcome the stranger,
turn from oppressive ways?
If we sing with joy
attending to our very words,
knowing the Lord in our midst,
we will be indestructible
even when our buildings fall to the ground.
Is it not time to welcome
our sisters and brothers

of all faiths
    and all nations
        and all ways loving
            and all classes
                and all variations of wellness?
                    Surely we can let ourselves be gathered anew . . .

TUESDAY

See, I am sending my messenger to prepare the way before me, and the Lord whom you seek will suddenly come to his temple. The messenger of the covenant in whom you delight—indeed, he is coming, says the Lord of hosts. But who can endure the day of his coming, and who can stand when he appears? For he is like a refiner's fire and like fullers' soap; he will sit as a refiner and purifier of silver, and he will purify the descendants of Levi and refine them like gold and silver, until they present offerings to the Lord in righteousness. Then the offering of Judah and Jerusalem will be pleasing to the Lord as in the days of old and as in former years.

—Malachi 3:1–4

REFINEMENT

snow falls today
the world is dusted
in winter white
early this season
a gift

I pause in my frantic
get-things-done pace
to notice the gentle flakes
dancing slowly
to settle here and there
in no hurry

muted grey edges
soften
the world seems
friendlier
quieter
and I've taken time to
notice the complexity of snow
and give thanks

WEDNESDAY

Again the Lord spoke to Ahaz, saying, "Ask a sign of the Lord your God; let it be deep as Sheol or high as heaven." But Ahaz said, "I will not ask, and I will not put the Lord to the test." Then Isaiah said: "Hear then, O house of David! Is it too little for you to weary mortals, that you weary my God also? Therefore the Lord himself will give you a sign. Look, the young woman is with child and shall bear a son, and shall name him Immanuel. He shall eat curds and honey by the time he knows how to refuse the evil and choose the good. For before the child knows how to refuse the evil and choose the good, the land before whose two kings you are in dread will be deserted. The Lord will bring on you and on your people and on your ancestral house such days as have not come since the day that Ephraim departed from Judah—the king of Assyria." On that day the Lord will whistle for the fly that is at the sources of the streams of Egypt, and for the bee that is in the land of Assyria. And they will all come and settle in the steep ravines, and in the clefts of the rocks, and on all the thorn bushes, and on all the pastures. On that day the Lord will shave with a razor hired beyond the River—with the king of Assyria—the head and the hair of the feet, and it will take off the beard as well. On that day one will keep alive a young cow and two sheep, and will eat curds because of the abundance of milk that they give; for everyone that is left in the land shall eat curds and honey. On that day every place where there used to be a thousand vines, worth a thousand shekels of silver, will become briers and thorns. With bow and arrows one will go there, for all the land will be briers and thorns; and as for all the hills that used to be hoed with a hoe, you will not go there for fear of briers and thorns; but they will become a place where cattle are let loose and where sheep tread.

—Isaiah 7:10–25

A HISTORY LESSON

Ahaz is a name seldom heard—
rarely referenced by the average person,
but one whose story ought to be known.
A powerful man who lost all control
in the name of easy peace
and personal success.

Who among us hasn't been fooled by
sparkling accolades and promises of more?
Ahaz trusted himself more than his God
and look where he landed—
captive to his enemies.

Believing his own wisdom over
words of the prophet in his midst,
Ahaz courted his enemies and
adapted his practices so as not to
stand alone as the alien
became familiar.

Little bits of ourselves, given away
in efforts to keep peace, make friends,
maintain authority add up
slowly dismantling all we hold dear
until we come up empty and overtaken,
lost—all control, complicated
illusion.

At the lowest point, comes the promise:
Emanuel to reclaim what was lost
and restore salvation to a nation

gone astray.
Ahaz may have forgotten, yet
You remember.

May we, too, remember You who stands
with us when we chase after shadows,
thinking them gods, or glittery trinkets,
believing them power.
Your promise may go unheeded but never undone.
Let us learn from Ahaz . . .

You who remember us whole even
as we break apart again and again.
Let us hear the words of the prophets
(from the days of old and in our midst)
that we may not be so repeatedly
fooled as to miss
Emanuel.

THURSDAY

But there will be no gloom for those who were in anguish. In the former time he brought into contempt the land of Zebulun and the land of Naphtali, but in the latter time he will make glorious the way of the sea, the land beyond the Jordan, Galilee of the nations. The people who walked in darkness have seen a great light; those who lived in a land of deep darkness—on them light has shined. You have multiplied the nation, you have increased its joy; they rejoice before you as with joy at the harvest, as people exult when dividing plunder. For the yoke of their burden, and the bar across their shoulders, the rod of their oppressor, you have broken as on the day of Midian. For all the boots of the tramping warriors and all the garments rolled in blood shall be burned as fuel for the fire. For a child has been born for us, a son given to us; authority rests upon his shoulders; and he is named Wonderful Counselor, Mighty God, Everlasting Father, Prince of Peace. His authority shall grow continually, and there shall be endless peace for the throne of David and his kingdom. He will establish and uphold it with justice and with righteousness from this time onward and forevermore. The zeal of the Lord of hosts will do this.

—Isaiah 9:1–7

A SESTINA FOR SEASONAL SHOPPERS

Darkness seems to gather, even in this season of light
days grow shorter, colder, as night strengthens her grasp.
So many people walk alone, hiding anguish, without hope,
waiting for something to change. Lights blink out cheer
while behind the decorated doors and windows
sadness frequently lurks with grief and anger blocking joy.

No one would guess the pain hidden in festive frenzy. Joy
is artificial in décor and faces when seen in the light.
Holiday wishes and synthetic snow grace shop windows
and walls while shoppers rush for sales and lose their grasp
on the season. It is not meant for false smiles and empty cheer,
but should truly set captives free to embrace the hope

of better days to come. But few seem to see or hear, and hope
slips further away. In the background someone sings of joy
and promise which seems to go unheard. Very little cheer
can be found here as worry brings heaviness, not light,
as time draws short. Readiness slips beyond reasonable grasp
and people barely glance up to notice the elaborate windows

with their merry displays. What would happen if windows
opened and revealed truth? If we spoke of a lack of hope
and the heaviness of despair? How hard it is to grasp
the intensity of the love that promises such boundless joy?
What if we say how afraid we are to walk in the light
and let go of our fears, make room for genuine cheer?

Would it bring us closer to acknowledge our struggle for cheer
or help us to see how similar we are behind closed windows
and doors? Surely we all walk in darkness and need light
as much (if not more) as ever before. How nice hope
would be if it could slow the hectic pace, make room for joy,
and place the fullness of meaning unavoidably within our grasp.

Wonderful Counselor. Mighty God. Impossible to grasp
Your coming among us. Everlasting Father. Surely You can cheer
us with this good news. Prince of Peace. You are the joy
of all nations and we want to hide behind curtained windows
instead of claim Your love for us. Yet You have not given up hope
in all the years between then and now. You call us to Your light

inviting us to truly grasp that nothing is hidden by our windows
or doors or false faces. Good cheer can be ours along with hope
if we but embrace Your joy, own our truth, and walk in the Light.

FRIDAY

The wilderness and the dry land shall be glad, the desert shall rejoice and blossom; like the crocus it shall blossom abundantly, and rejoice with joy and singing. The glory of Lebanon shall be given to it, the majesty of Carmel and Sharon. They shall see the glory of the Lord, the majesty of our God. Strengthen the weak hands, and make firm the feeble knees. Say to those who are of a fearful heart, "Be strong, do not fear! Here is your God. He will come with vengeance, with terrible recompense. He will come and save you."

—Isaiah 35:1–4

A REMEMBRANCE

I remember my own days of disbelief
      chaos of the wilderness
      scorching heat of the desert
      fear and trembling
      hiding in shadows
Sometimes the dark days seem unbearably close

It was hard to believe in abundance
      knowing hardship
      wandering sightlessly
      worrying endlessly
      misunderstanding everything
It is a wonder I can sing at all now (let alone with joy)

This season with its promises and its waiting
      rekindles old yearnings
      stirs the places of emptiness
      tempts me with counterfeit hopes
      conjures images of what might have been
Holding fast to Your presence is not always easy

Yet when Your glory shines in and through me
      wilderness and desert blossom into life
      fear and yearning give way to Your strength
      worry and emptiness burst into rejoicing song
      today's temptations wither in Your hands
I know the joys of Your salvation

Come
   Quickly
      Here
         Now
            Again

SATURDAY

A shoot shall come out from the stump of Jesse, and a branch shall grow out of his roots. The spirit of the Lord shall rest on him, the spirit of wisdom and understanding, the spirit of counsel and might, the spirit of knowledge and the fear of the Lord. His delight shall be in the fear of the Lord. He shall not judge by what his eyes see, or decide by what his ears hear; but with righteousness he shall judge the poor, and decide with equity for the meek of the earth; he shall strike the earth with the rod of his mouth, and with the breath of his lips he shall kill the wicked. Righteousness shall be the belt around his waist, and faithfulness the belt around his loins. The wolf shall live with the lamb, the leopard shall lie down with the kid, the calf and the lion and the fatling together, and a little child shall lead them. The cow and the bear shall graze, their young shall lie down together; and the lion shall eat straw like the ox. The nursing child shall play over the hole of the asp, and the weaned child shall put its hand on the adder's den. They will not hurt or destroy on all my holy mountain; for the earth will be full of the knowledge of the Lord as the waters cover the sea.

—Isaiah 11:1–9

A SACRED PLACE

a cold, clammy grayness
   slithers over the beach
      as the sun takes her leave

         all others who've come to walk
            have gone with the faint warmth
            of day quickly fading

                  I am alone on the shore
                   as night spreads over
                        sandflats and tidal pools

                 gulls cry overhead
               the tide rhythmically ebbs lower
               mist silently gathers in

             I stand in awe of the power
         a life-force neither good nor ill
     beyond comprehension and control

        my solitary walk along receding waters
          washes away worry and distraction
            filling me with peace

                 reminding me of innocent days
                   when You were the ocean
                     to my way of knowing

             all-powerful
             ever-constant
          always changing

sustaining life
taking life
at seeming random

essential
unfathomable
mysterious

now the ocean is my sacred space
a place of peace and joy
perspective and promise renewing

in all seasons I seek You here
in the quiet, uncrowded hours
needing time alone with You

as this day ends, meet me here
remind me of lost innocence
and half-forgotten promises

so when the tide turns
I will be refilled with the joy
of knowing You

Love

"For the mountains may depart and the hills be removed, but my steadfastlove shall not depart from you, and my covenant of peace shall not be removed, says the Lord, who has compassion on you."

—Isaiah 54:10

SUNDAY

Here is my servant, whom I uphold, my chosen, in whom my soul delights; I have put my spirit upon him; he will bring forth justice to the nations. He will not cry or lift up his voice, or make it heard in the street; a bruised reed he will not break, and a dimly burning wick he will not quench; he will faithfully bring forth justice. He will not grow faint or be crushed until he has established justice in the earth; and the coastlands wait for his teaching. Thus says God, the Lord, who created the heavens and stretched them out, who spread out the earth and what comes from it, who gives breath to the people upon it and spirit to those who walk in it: I am the Lord, I have called you in righteousness, I have taken you by the hand and kept you; I have given you as a covenant to the people, a light to the nations, to open the eyes that are blind, to bring out the prisoners from the dungeon, from the prison those who sit in darkness. I am the Lord, that is my name; my glory I give to no other, nor my praise to idols. See, the former things have come to pass, and new things I now declare; before they spring forth, I tell you of them. Sing to the Lord a new song, his praise from the end of the earth! Let the sea roar and all that fills it, the coastlands and their inhabitants. Let the desert and its towns lift up their voice, the villages that Kedar inhabits; let the inhabitants of Sela sing for joy, let them shout from the tops of the mountains. Let them give glory to the Lord, and declare his praise in the coastlands.

—Isaiah 42:1–12

BREATH TO THE PEOPLE

Breathe again on Your people
and fill us with a new spirit.

        We are caught in former things–
                a covenant frequently forgotten
                nations dimmed by war
                eyes blinded by fear
                prisoners held in ignorance–
        we are in need of a new song.

I long for the justice of Your breath
and the strength of Your promise.

        I grow weary of waiting day after day—
                the desert is at war with the mountains
                the villages and the coastlands tremble
                while fear darkens the land
                making sister and brother appear other—
        my voice breaks under the weight.

Let us be the delight of Your soul
following the One who establishes integrity.

        In the light of Your love–
                a covenant brings life
                nations learn peace
                eyes open hearts
                captives find release–
        Your people sing a new song.

Breathe again on Your people
and fill us with a new spirit.

MONDAY

O Lord, our Sovereign, how majestic is your name in all the earth! You have set your glory above the heavens. Out of the mouths of babes and infants you have founded a bulwark because of your foes, to silence the enemy and the avenger. When I look at your heavens, the work of your fingers, the moon and the stars that you have established; what are human beings that you are mindful of them, mortals that you care for them? Yet you have made them a little lower than God, and crowned them with glory and honor. You have given them dominion over the works of your hands; you have put all things under their feet, all sheep and oxen, and also the beasts of the field, the birds of the air, and the fish of the sea, whatever passes along the paths of the seas. O Lord, our Sovereign, how majestic is your name in all the earth!

—Psalm 8:1–9

For God so loved the world that he gave his only Son, so that everyone who believes in him may not perish but may have eternal life. Indeed, God did not send the Son into the world to condemn the world, but in order that the world might be saved through him. Those who believe in him are not condemned; but those who do not believe are condemned already, because they have not believed in the name of the only Son of God. And this is the judgment, that the light has come into the world, and people loved darkness rather than light because their deeds were evil. For all who do evil hate the light and do not come to the light, so that their deeds may not be exposed. But those who do what is true come to the light, so that it may be clearly seen that their deeds have been done in God.

—John 3:16–21

PROFOUND INSIGHT

in the light of the moon
at the ocean's edge
seeking the moment when
horizon meets darkness

under countless stars
on innumerable grains of sand
awed by the vastness
of the universe

I am mind full
and wonder that You
who created all that is
would take notice of me

Your majesty and power
fill me with awe
and confront me
with transforming truth

You so loved the world
that I may walk in light
through the darkness
bearing Your honor and glory

the moon and stars
adorn night skies
a thousand miracles
are a handful of sand

You've done all this and still

You love the particularity of me
asking only that I love
with Your love in return

A gift You deem me
worthy to receive
without hesitation
You make me whole

In gratitude and awe
I lift my voice with
ancient words of
gratefulness and praise

O Lord, our Sovereign,
how majestic is
Your name
in all the earth!

TUESDAY

Comfort, O comfort my people, says your God. Speak tenderly to Jerusalem, and cry to her that she has served her term, that her penalty is paid, that she has received from the Lord's hand double for all her sins. A voice cries out: "In the wilderness prepare the way of the Lord, make straight in the desert a highway for our God. Every valley shall be lifted up, and every mountain and hill be made low; the uneven ground shall become level, and the rough places a plain. Then the glory of the Lord shall be revealed, and all people shall see it together, for the mouth of the Lord has spoken."

—Isaiah 40:1–5

ADVENT WORDS

H oliday lights glittering inside and out
O ffering happy colors in the night,
P ointing toward the Light,
E ncouraging waiting on tiptoe.

P rophecies of promise
E choing through music–
A ncient and new (harmonious and not quite so)
C alling all to reclaim, remember,
E mbody "Good will to all on earth."

J umping up and down
O nly because
Y ou live.

L amenting no more . . .
O pening to life anew . . .
V aluing all (without exception) . . .
E manuel.

WEDNESDAY

A voice says, "Cry out!" And I said, "What shall I cry?" All people are grass, their constancy is like the flower of the field. The grass withers, the flower fades, when the breath of the Lord blows upon it; surely the people are grass. The grass withers, the flower fades; but the word of our God will stand forever. Get you up to a high mountain, O Zion, herald of good tidings; lift up your voice with strength, O Jerusalem, herald of good tidings, lift it up, do not fear; say to the cities of Judah, "Here is your God!" See, the Lord God comes with might, and his arm rules for him; his reward is with him, and his recompense before him. He will feed his flock like a shepherd; he will gather the lambs in his arms, and carry them in his bosom, and gently lead the mother sheep.

—Isaiah 40:6–11

OUT CRY

The nights are filled with tears
wrought through inconstancy
and the withering and fading
of timid hope.

        Who will cry out for You?

Echoing into daylight
war reverberates destruction
and disturbance, damaging
potential peace.

        Who will cry out for You?

Good tidings lose strength
when fear solidifies distance
between brother and sister,
silencing joy.

        Who will cry out for You?

Knowing our frailty, You
call to us, inviting us,
holding out Your arms
in welcoming love.

        Who will cry out for You?

The grass withers.
The flowers fade.
The One who is to come
stands forever.

Will you cry out?

THURSDAY

Praise the Lord! Praise, O servants of the Lord; praise the name of the Lord. Blessed be the name of the Lord from this time on and forevermore. From the rising of the sun to its setting the name of the Lord is to be praised. The Lord is high above all nations, and his glory above the heavens. Who is like the Lord our God, who is seated on high, who looks far down on the heavens and the earth? He raises the poor from the dust, and lifts the needy from the ash heap, to make them sit with princes, with the princes of his people. He gives the barren woman a home, making her the joyous mother of children. Praise the Lord!

—Psalm 113

In the beginning was the Word, and the Word was with God, and the Word was God. He was in the beginning with God. All things came into being through him, and without him not one thing came into being. What has come into being in him was life, and the life was the light of all people. The light shines in the darkness, and the darkness did not overcome it. There was a man sent from God, whose name was John. He came as a witness to testify to the light, so that all might believe through him. He himself was not the light, but he came to testify to the light. The true light, which enlightens everyone, was coming into the world.

—John 1:1–9

LIGHT SHINES

From the rising of the sun . . .

When prayers uttered in desperation
linger, unheard, unanswered,
praise comes hard
at the rise of the sun.

How many times has the dark of night
brought longing and pleading
for a child who would bring light?
My one lingering regret.

And then she took my hand
and whispered her tearful secrets
of shame and horror
asking me to reassure her.

So much trust in her little tearstained
face turned to me with such hope
for help, safety, acceptance . . .
I would not turn away.

I am not childless.
Your children are my children
and they come to me,
looking for You.

How could I have thought
myself barren when entrusted
with such gifts as a small hand
in mine seeking refuge?

Light shines even in my darkness
as You answered my prayers
patiently waiting for me to notice
the joyous home of Your love.

As the sun rises, outshining
regret, I will sing Your praises

                              . . . to its setting.

FRIDAY

God is our refuge and strength, a very present help in trouble. Therefore we will not fear, though the earth should change, though the mountains shake in the heart of the sea; though its waters roar and foam, though the mountains tremble with its tumult. There is a river whose streams make glad the city of God, the holy habitation of the Most High. God is in the midst of the city; it shall not be moved; God will help it when the morning dawns. The nations are in an uproar, the kingdoms totter; he utters his voice, the earth melts. The Lord of hosts is with us; the God of Jacob is our refuge. Come, behold the works of the Lord; see what desolations he has brought on the earth. He makes wars cease to the end of the earth; he breaks the bow, and shatters the spear; he burns the shields with fire. "Be still, and know that I am God! I am exalted among the nations, I am exalted in the earth." The Lord of hosts is with us; the God of Jacob is our refuge.

—Psalm 46

A highway shall be there, and it shall be called the Holy Way; the unclean shall not travel on it, but it shall be for God's people; no traveler, not even fools, shall go astray. No lion shall be there, nor shall any ravenous beast come up on it; they shall not be found there, but the redeemed shall walk there. And the ransomed of the Lord shall return, and come to Zion with singing; everlasting joy shall be upon their heads; they shall obtain joy and gladness, and sorrow and sighing shall flee away.

—Isaiah 35:8–10

A HOLY WAY

When will we be still and listen?
We busy ourselves with so little
that matters, sowing more discord
than peace.

You make no distinction among the nations,
fools and travelers alike are invited to find
asylum in You, obtaining joy and gladness
along the way.

Left to our own devises we build dividing
lines, weapons of destruction, definitions
of deserving, and roadblocks for any
seeking justice.

You proclaim something else entirely
breaking bows and bombs, ending war,
naming all redeemed, dismantling
our differences.

We are in trouble, believing we can stop
tumultuous times with weapons of safety
and wars of justice, seeking refuge in
lesser gods.

Still You welcome fools. Teach us
to be still in the uproar, letting sorrow
and sighing flee from Your presence
right now.

Let us make a Holy Way in our midst
where all may find refuge and strength.

CHRISTMAS EVE

But you, O Bethlehem of Ephrathah, who are one of the little clans of Judah, from you shall come forth for me one who is to rule in Israel, whose origin is from of old, from ancient days. Therefore he shall give them up until the time when she who is in labor has brought forth; then the rest of his kindred shall return to the people of Israel. And he shall stand and feed his flock in the strength of the Lord, in the majesty of the name of the Lord his God. And they shall live secure, for now he shall be great to the ends of the earth; and he shall be the one of peace.

—Micah 5:2–5a

In those days Mary set out and went with haste to a Judean town in the hill country, where she entered the house of Zechariah and greeted Elizabeth. When Elizabeth heard Mary's greeting, the child leaped in her womb. And Elizabeth was filled with the Holy Spirit and exclaimed with a loud cry, "Blessed are you among women, and blessed is the fruit of your womb. And why has this happened to me, that the mother of my Lord comes to me? For as soon as I heard the sound of your greeting, the child in my womb leaped for joy. And blessed is she who believed that there would be a fulfillment of what was spoken to her by the Lord." And Mary said, "My soul magnifies the Lord, and my spirit rejoices in God my Savior, for he has looked with favor on the lowliness of his servant. Surely, from now on all generations will call me blessed; for the Mighty One has done great things for me, and holy is his name. His mercy is for those who fear him from generation to generation. He has shown strength with his arm; he has scattered the proud in the thoughts of their hearts. He has brought down the powerful from their thrones, and lifted up the lowly; he has filled the hungry with good things, and sent the rich away empty. He has helped his servant Israel, in remembrance of his mercy, according to the promise he made to our ancestors, to Abraham and to his descendants forever."

—Luke 1:39–55

BETHLEHEM AWAITS

I stand in my usual place
and You point me to a distant city on a far horizon,
telling me that Bethlehem beckons weary travelers
in this season of watchful expectation.
    The streets are paved with history
        scarred with struggle, loss, and utter despair.
        So, too, filled in with joy, hope, and life
    if any care to look.

    In the quiet of the night
    in the dark forgotten places
    I might hear echoes of Rachel
    weeping for her children–
        the innocent ones lost
        and the strong ones sacrificed–
    You tell me her tears fall
    still.

If I am quiet enough to listen,
the shadows of dusk will whisper of battles
    won and lost
        lives taken and given
            names little remembered
                and stories seldom told.

        In the darkening alleyways I might encounter
        a remembrance of days gone by–
            the days of strong, victorious kings and prophets
            or sadder times when even the priests were led astray.

If I walk through the city,
around an unexpected corner

faint music could touch my ears,
the joy of David dancing before the Lord
    unhidden,
    unashamed,
a welcome sight for a city long in need.

You call me from where I stand,
with a promise:
On the other side of the cold barren lands,
    hot scorching deserts,
        high mountains,
            desolate wilderness
                this little city awaits–
                    with all its joys and sorrows
                    built into its walls and alleyways–
                to bring light and hope once more.

                Even now
                while I am reluctant to move
                shepherds mind their flocks and
                a homeless family seeks shelter for a night.

The journey can be long and hard
    but for those who go
        Bethlehem holds a chance
            to weep with Rachel
            dance with David
                leap for joy
                    or kneel before a manger
                        as we encounter You.

City lights glimmer on a distant horizon;
I am setting out.

    Bethlehem awaits.

Christmas Day

In those days a decree went out from Emperor Augustus that all the world should be registered. This was the first registration and was taken while Quirinius was governor of Syria. All went to their own towns to be registered. Joseph also went from the town of Nazareth in Galilee to Judea, to the city of David called Bethlehem, because he was descended from the house and family of David. He went to be registered with Mary, to whom he was engaged and who was expecting a child. While they were there, the time came for her to deliver her child. And she gave birth to her firstborn son and wrapped him in bands of cloth, and laid him in a manger, because there was no place for them in the inn. In that region there were shepherds living in the fields, keeping watch over their flock by night. Then an angel of the Lord stood before them, and the glory of the Lord shone around them, and they were terrified. But the angel said to them, "Do not be afraid; for see– I am bringing you good news of great joy for all the people: to you is born this day in the city of David a Savior, who is the Messiah, the Lord. This will be a sign for you: you will find a child wrapped in bands of cloth and lying in a manger." And suddenly there was with the angel a multitude of the heavenly host, praising God and saying, "Glory to God in the highest heaven, and on earth peace among those whom he favors!" When the angels had left them and gone into heaven, the shepherds said to one another, "Let us go now to Bethlehem and see this thing that has taken place, which the Lord has made known to us." So they went with haste and found Mary and Joseph, and the child lying in the manger. When they saw this, they made known what had been told them about this child; and all who heard it were amazed at what the shepherds told them. But Mary treasured all these words and pondered them in her heart. The shepherds returned, glorifying and praising God for all they had heard and seen, as it had been told them.

—Luke 2:1–20

GOOD NEWS

How familiar, this story of birth—
no vacancy fails to register
along with the musky manger scene
(never mind a frightful angel
with his accompanying heavenly host).
Instead we see Sunday school children
dressed as adorable stars, pudgy shepherds
herding thumb-sucking sheep
guided by angels with tilting tinseled halos.
Off key enthusiasm marks the heralding
of good news sung out while a very young
Mary hushes a baby who doesn't grasp
the sacredness of the moment.

But do we hear this controversial story?
The overcrowded city, the dark cave
complete with animals and feeding trough?
Do we quake with the shepherds at the sight
of an angel filling the sky with good news?
Can we marvel at the mystery of the star
that marked the scene, amazing all?
In a moment of innocence, will we ponder
with Mary the incomprehensible instant
of incarnation when everything changed?

It is not too late for us to bear witness
to the wonder and awe that fills this day—
Take note of the messy manger scene,
tremble with shepherds, and hurry
to see for ourselves the improbability
of promise born into life anew

this very day proclaiming good news
that never ends when we take notice
glorifying God with praises, embracing
joy and peace for the sake of all God's
people, no exceptions—God *is* with us.
This is the Good News.
Amen.

Reader's Guide

The purpose of this guide is to offer questions that promote deeper thought or conversation. If you are using this guide during your personal Advent journey, you may choose to spend some time with each of these questions or choose the one for each poem that has most meaning for you. If the individual poems raise other questions for you, pursue those. Go where the poem leads in terms of thought, feelings, and insights. There is no wrong way to contemplate poetry.

I chose to write poetry because its language is similar to that of theology. Poetry is allusive; it points toward a truth with image and metaphor. So, too, theology; it points to a larger Truth. In this case, the poems are theological in that they are addressed to God, or raise issues of the human spirit's longing to be more deeply connected to the Holy Spirit. They do so with layers of meaning which may be shuffled and reshuffled over time as our understanding and relationship with God changes, deepens, and transforms us. But do not approach them with fear or doubt. Read and listen and let the meaning emerge for you.

If you are using this guide to lead a church group, there are some options. Participants can reflect on these questions (and others the poems may raise) and bring these responses to the group. In addition or as another option, these questions can be answered on a community or congregational level. This could provoke some interesting conversation and you may choose one or two poems to guide discussion as time allows.

These questions can be used daily to inspire journaling or personal prayer. Or they can be used to enhance a discussion of the weekly themes. Hope, Peace, Joy, and Love are the tradition themes of Advent dating back many centuries. I chose to use them to for this book because I believe they still capture the essence of the season and are worthy of our attention. At a time when depression and other mental health issues affect a growing majority of people, what better to look for than the Hope birthed in a manger? When war and violence dominates the evening news, who does not yearn for the Peace proclaimed by angel voices? With the false promises of a consumer-driven society, the Joy of Emanuel (God-with-us) is a much-needed experience. And as we live at a dizzying pace that distorts our understanding of ourselves and one another, who would not benefit from a reminder of God's Love for all humanity?

As you read the poems and the questions pertaining to them, do not be afraid to find your own meaning in the words. Though it may be tempting to wonder what I was thinking when I wrote, this is less helpful than examining thoughts and feelings evoked in you the reader(s). If you are inclined to head in this direction, then you could look for how the poem relates to the scripture(s) it draws on. Some of these are more obvious than others and could lead to remarkable conversations.

However you choose to use this guide, may you find Light for your journey and hope enough to keep the dark at bay . . .

Week One: HOPE

Re-Vision

1. Have you ever had an experience of doubting God's presence (maybe on a smaller, or less dramatic scale than Zechariah)? If so, what got in the way of seeing God more clearly?

2. Have any traditions become routine enough to have lost sacred meaning?

3. What hopes do you have for this Advent season? In other words, what are you waiting for?

Then and Now

1. Have you experienced or witnessed injustice? What happened? How did you feel?

2. Is there something that prevents you from experiencing Hope this Advent season? What might change this for you?

3. What, if anything, would you like to tell others about how you experience God's presence in the world today?

4. Is there anything you can or want to do to make Advent more meaningful for you?

Prepare Ye the Way

1. Are there any experiences from your past that still feel unresolved in ways that negatively affect you?

2. Do you have a list of things to be done that prevent you from being able to relax and enjoy the season?

3. Is there anything you wish you had time for that would feel restful?

Broken Hope

1. Have you had times of waking up in the middle of the night worried over something? If so, what kinds of worries cause you to lose sleep?

2. Have you ever lost hope? If you have, what helped restore it?

3. Do you have any particular hopes for this Advent season?

Human Ways

1. Where have you turned from God?

2. How can you do "something new"?

3. How can you bring or restore value to another person?

A Sonnet for Hope

1. Have you ever made a bad choice even though your intentions were good? What happened? How did it work out?

2. If you have had times of feeling lost and unsure of yourself, did anyone help you get through it? What was it like? What helped you?

3. When do you feel yourself cradled in God's love? What can you do to share this with others?

Of Promise and Grace

1. Have you experienced barrenness or emptiness in your life? What kept you from finding hope at these times?

2. Are you in need of new life now? What fears or doubts get in the way of embracing possibility?

3. Sometimes good news comes from unexpected sources and significantly changes our lives for the better. Have you had this experience? What happened?

Week 2: PEACE

Advent Again

1. Do you have any laments to bring before God this Advent season? If so, what are they?

2. What, if anything, prevents you from experiencing peace?

3. Have you noticed God's presence in a particular way? What was that like? What, if anything, will draw your attention to God's presence during this Advent season?

Words of the Prophets

1. Do you have dreams or desires that distract you from God? What are they?

2. Are you likely to pursue something other than peace? If you are, what is it and why do you think you want it?

3. In what ways might God be waiting patiently for you?

A Quiet Lament

1. Do you feel like you are far from God or close to God or somewhere in the middle? What makes you feel this way? Would you like your relationship with God to be different? In what ways?

2. Where do you experience awe of God?

3. What, if anything, breaks your heart? Is there any kind of ignorance or madness that you would like to see come to an end?

4. Is there anything that makes you feel cynical? If there is something that makes you feel this way, can you or anyone else change it? Why or why not?

A Promise Remembered

1. Do you have a desire that distracts you from things you think are important? If so, what is it and how does it distract you?

2. Do you feel vulnerable or fragile in some way? If so, what helps you to feel more safe and secure when you experience or are reminded of your vulnerability?

3. What would it feel like to live in God's "city of beauty, security, and justice"? What would this look like in day to day life?

A Villanelle for Advent (a Villanelle is a classic form of poetry, with set rhyme and meter)

1. Have you experienced a loss or a deep sense of regret? If you have, do you feel this more keenly at this time of year? How does it affect you? What helps you feel better?

2. Do you feel confined or closed in in any way or in any aspect of your life? (Work? Home? Family?) If so, can you do anything to change it? Do you want to change it?

3. What is your prayer as you wait for the peace of Christ to come anew?

Storm Watch

1. Does anything obscure hope for you? If so, what is it that gets in your way? How does it prevent you from having hope?

2. If you have experienced hopelessness, was there someone who held hope for you during that time? If so, what was that like?

3. Is there a place where you find peace? An actual place? A particular spiritual practice or ritual? Is it something you can share with others? What would that be like for you?

A Prayer for Peace

1. Do you have need of refuge and shelter at this point in your life? If so, what is it that causes you to feel in need of rest?

2. Are you in need of forgiveness? Why or why not? Do you need to offer forgiveness to someone who has wronged or offended you? If so, will you offer it? Why or why not?

3. What does walking in the "way of peace" mean for you?

Week 3: JOY

The Third Candle

1. Have you experienced betrayal? If you have, what happened? Have you healed or recovered? If so, how did that happen? If not, what gets in the way of healing?

2. Have you experienced good coming out of something terrible? If so, what happened and what was the good?

3. What, if anything, do you think would increase joy in your life?

4. Do you need to begin again with God? Why or why not?

Regathering

1. Have you ever let someone down when it really mattered? If so, what was that like? Has anyone ever let you down when it really mattered? If so, what was that like?

2. Is there any part of your life where you need joy? If so, in what way? And what gets in your way of experiencing joy?

3. This poem speaks of allowing ourselves to be "gathered anew" by God. What does this mean to you? How might such an experience change you?

Refinement

1. This poem speaks of snow as a gift, a reminder to slow down and notice the wonders of creation. Have you received any similar kinds of gifts? If you have, what was the gift and what did it do for you?

2. Do you need to slow down and notice the world around you? If you do, what might get in the way? How might you go about slowing down a bit?

3. What fills you with gratitude?

A History Lesson

1. Ahaz made some bad choices because he failed to listen to the advice offered him. Have you ever had an experience of making a bad choice or dismissing good advice? If you have, what happened? What resulted?

2. Have you given away any parts of yourself? If you have, what did you think was the purpose or did you only notice later? Have you been able to reclaim those parts?

3. What does it mean for you to have a God who knows you as you are and claims you as God's own beloved child?

A Sestina for Seasonal Shoppers (Sestina is a classic form of poetry with a set order for the six ending words in each stanza)

1. Does anything prevent you from enjoying this season of preparation? If anything does, what is it and why?

2. Does anything hinder your participation in the joy of the season? If so, what is it and can you change it?

3. Where or how do you make room for joy during Advent? throughout the rest of the year?

A Remembrance

1. Have you lived through "days of disbelief"? If you have, how were those days different from now? Were they different from now?

2. Do any temptations from your past hold power for you now? If so, what are they?

3. Do you experience, or have you experienced, God's glory shining in and through you? If you do, what is that like? How does it make you feel?

A Sacred Place

1. Where do you find renewal? What about this particular place is renewing for you?

2. How does a visit to this place affect you?

3. Do you experience, or have you experienced, the joy of knowing God? What is this like for you?

Week 4: LOVE

Breath to the People

1. Do you need God to breathe a new spirit into you? If so, in what way?

2. What, if anything, makes you weary?

3. What, if anything, would you like to change about the way you live your life?

Profound Insight

1. Have you experienced God's love for the particularity of you? If you have, what was this like?

2. Have you tried to love with that same love? If you have, in what way? How did it feel?

3. Is there anything you need in order to lift your voice with gratitude and praise? If so what is it and how can this need be met?

Advent Words

1. Do you get excited while waiting for good things? If you do what kind of things fill you with delighted anticipation?

2. What is your favorite Christmas Carol or Advent hymn? What do you like about this particular hymn?

3. What makes you want to jump up and down for joy?

4. How do you know God loves you?

Out Cry

1. Does anything make you want to cry out for God's response? If so, what is it that upsets, angers or saddens you enough to want God to do something?

2. If there are things that make you want to ask God "why!?" Do you? Or are there reasons that you don't? What do you think would happen if you did cry out to God?

3. Do you think God is saddened, angered, or pained over anything? If so what and why?

Light Shines

1. Have you had prayers you thought were unanswered? Have you been surprised at discovering an unexpected answer? If you have, how long did it take you to notice the answer and why?

2. This poem speaks of an unexpected answer to prayer and the gifts from God discovered there. Do you believe God has entrusted you with any similar gifts? If you do, what are they?

3. Do you notice the joyous home of God's love? If you do, when or what draws your attention to God?

A Holy Way

1. Does anything keep you too busy to be still and listen? If things do, what are they?

2. Do you think God's way differs from your way? If you do, why do you think this and how is God's way different from yours?

3. Is there anyone or group of people God welcomes that make you uncomfortable? If there is, who is it? Do you know what it is about these people that makes it difficult for you to welcome them as children of God?

4. Do you have any despair, sadness or sorrow, that you would like to leave with God this Advent? If you do, what might help you let it go and make room for healing?

Bethlehem Awaits

1. Advent can be described as metaphoric journey to Bethlehem. We spend four weeks preparing for the coming of Christ. As you have traveled through Advent, have you encountered difficulty? Has anything prevented you from experiencing a deeper sense of God's presence this year? If so, what was it that got in the way for you?

2. Does Bethlehem hold promises for you? If it does, what is it?

3. Do you arrive at the manger, in the presence of the Christ with a particular need? If you do, what is it?

Good News

1. Is there a part of the Christmas story that is hard for you to believe or accept? If there is, what is it and why?

2. Do you bear witness to the coming of Christ into the world? If you do, how do you do it or what do you do?

3. Do you notice anything new this Christmas?

Scripture Index

OLD TESTAMENT

Psalm 5:11   45
Psalm 8   69
Psalm 33:22   19
Psalm 46   80
Psalm 85:10   23
Psalm 113   77

Isaiah 2:2–4   25
Isaiah 4:2–6   42
Isaiah 7:10–25   54
Isaiah 9:1–7   57
Isaiah 11:10–9   62
Isaiah 12:2–6   47
Isaiah 29:13–24   31
Isaiah 33:17–22   34
Isaiah 35:1–4   60
Isaiah 35:5–7   37
Isaiah 35:8–10   80
Isaiah 40:1–5   70
Isaiah 40:6–11   74
Isaiah 42:1–2   67
Isaiah 42:5–9   18
Isaiah 54:10   65
Isaiah 60:1–4   xv

Jeremiah 33:14–16   13

Jeremiah 33:19–26   16

Amos 2:1–8   28
Amos 5:18–27   6

Micah 5:2   82

Zephaniah 3:14–20   49

Malachi 3:1–4   52
Malachi 4:1–6   10

NEW TESTAMENT

Luke 1:5–25   4
Luke 1:26–38   7
Luke 1:39–55   83
Luke 1:57–66   20
Luke 1:68–80   42
Luke 2:1–20   87
Luke 3:1–6   10

John 1:1–9   77
John 1:6–13   28
John 3:16–21   69
John 5:30–38   39